I Was a Bell

I Was a Bell

poems

M. Soledad Caballero

2019
Red Hen Press
Benjamin Saltman
Award

 Red Hen Press | *Pasadena, CA*

Book layout by Daniela Connor

Library of Congress Cataloging-in-Publication Data

Names: Caballero, M. Soledad, 1973– author.
Title: I was a bell : poems / M. Soledad Caballero.
Description: Pasadena, CA : Red Hen Press, [2021]
Identifiers: LCCN 2021014245 (print) | LCCN 2021014246 (ebook) | ISBN
  9781597094900 (trade paperback) | ISBN 9781597094962 (epub)
Subjects: LCGFT: Poetry.
Classification: LCC PS3603.A26 I26 2021 (print) | LCC PS3603.A26 (ebook)
  | DDC 811/.6—dc23
LC record available at https://lccn.loc.gov/2021014245
LC ebook record available at https://lccn.loc.gov/2021014246

Publication of this book has been made possible in part through the financial support of Jim Wilson.

The National Endowment for the Arts, the Los Angeles County Arts Commission, the Ahmanson Foundation, the Dwight Stuart Youth Fund, the Max Factor Family Foundation, the Pasadena Tournament of Roses Foundation, the Pasadena Arts & Culture Commission and the City of Pasadena Cultural Affairs Division, the City of Los Angeles Department of Cultural Affairs, the Audrey & Sydney Irmas Charitable Foundation, the Meta & George Rosenberg Foundation, the Albert and Elaine Borchard Foundation, the Adams Family Foundation, Amazon Literary Partnership, the Sam Francis Foundation, and the Mara W. Breech Foundation partially support Red Hen Press.

First Edition
Published by Red Hen Press
www.redhen.org

ACKNOWLEDGMENTS

The author would like to thank the editors of the following publications in which some of these poems first appeared.

Arts and Letters, a Journal of Contemporary Culture: "Flight"; *Barzakh Literary Magazine*: "Rooted"; *Bone Bouquet*: "Villa Grimaldi"; *Crab Orchard*: "Immigration Office, Oklahoma City, Oklahoma 1985"; *Memorious*: "The Generals of South America," "You Have to Leave Me Twice"; *Memoryhouse*: "Pacific Dreams," "The Order of Things"; *Mob Queens House*: "La Doncella"; *Origins Journal*: "I Was a Bell," "Someday I Will Visit Hawk Mountain," "To Document"; *Pilgrimage*: "Birds of Prey," "In the Time of the Patriarch"; *Quarry*: "After the Election: A Father Speaks to His Son"; *River Styx*: "Ode to My Hair"; *SWWIM*: "To the Boys Who Bully My Nephew in the Sixth Grade"; *The Acentos Review*: "What Remains Buried"; *The Florida Review*: "My English Decades"; *The Mississippi Review*: "Confessions"; *The Missouri Review*: "Losing Spanish"; *The Pittsburgh Poetry Review*: "Marriage"; *The Pittsburgh Post-Gazette*: "Alien Magic"; *The Rumpus*: "In the Poison Time There is Love," "What You are Doing is Living"; and *Uppagus*: "When You Go Out to Walk the Dog" (as "How I know this is love").

"Before Intersectionality" appeared in *Introduction to Women's, Gender, and Sexuality Studies* (Oxford University Press, 2017). "The Spell" appeared in *Feminist and Queer Theory: An Intersectional and Transnational Reader* (Oxford University Press, 2020).

CONTENTS

Bird Girl

Waiting for the Horsemen

I Was a Bell

Flight Plan

Para las mujeres de mi alma
Ester, Irma, Javiera, Macarena, Montserrat, Natalia, y Silvia

I Was a Bell

Bird Girl

Losing Spanish

She speaks a gringa Spanish
like mine but without the trill in the *R*'s
a bit too much throat around the vowels,
a soft tongue no anchoring against teeth,
her sounds too open, too big
for the sinews of Spanish.
This makes sense. She's five
years younger than me, grew up
on a prairie where snow falls
flat and thick, a world of white,
of strange monsters made of steel
dragons hungry for black sludge.
She played in Oklahoma fields,
a skinny fleck of a girl, in a secondhand
pink parka, scarlet hat and gloves, a burst
of color against the cold.
Lanky, fast, she twirled her body,
a bird of paradise dancing against
the stark flatness of the plains.
Unlike me, she laughed, shouted, lived
in a wilderness of ice,
unaware of other snow in the mountains,
tall peaks cutting into sky,
reminders that something is
beautiful in a thin southern country
where the color of blood ruled
the rivers, the streets, the night,
where boots marched in the rhythm
of sadness and steel alongside tanks.
Seven thousand miles away she lived
unaware of cement graves in stadiums,
purple and black of bodies
disappeared after electricity,
the General's timid smile radiating

death in that other country.
In the Oklahoma panhandle,
she did not remember the sirens,
the curfews, the fear reeking.
She had no memories burned
into muscles, no sounds, no
echoes or language of sadness
She grew up in a world of frozen water,
with brightness of snow
with nothing to forget,
she lost Spanish.

Birds of Prey

I.

My first bird was a dove, but I did not know it.
In Abuela's birdcage, I held it, hatched new out
of an eggshell the color of sand. She had many
birds with feathers light and thin, like fingers.
The partridges in their regal browns and grays.
The songbirds, specks of voice and dance, bright reds,
vivid yellows, oranges, like the sun over the Pacific.
Doves in pairs, with wide eyes and wheat-colored
wings, nested in the upper shelves of the cage.
Her birds seemed infinite and wild. They lived in
the walk-in cage, separated by wood and wires. They
sang into dusk, a gaggle of voices, waited for escape.

II.

Some days, I hid in the cage. The ground smelled of wet
straw and bird shit. I sat next to the birdfeed, cupped
the body of my bird in my hands, a talisman of heat
and eyes. It wrestled helplessly. Head jerking in jagged
circles. Its beak a dark stone, an arrow moving to find
flesh, jab a blood wound into my seven-year-old hand.
But I was firm. I wanted its secrets, its love. I was a patient
warden. Somewhere in the bird's bones was magic,
a spell at least, an incantation, a melody to break the General,
his hard smile. The bird was my weapon. Abuela's gentle
fingers peeled away mine. My grasp was rough. Her whispers
soft. She said *déjalo ir, mijita*. But I needed its fragile
warmth, its breath inside my skin. I was young, knew little
of the world and its poisons. But I sensed emptiness and fear.
The soul missing from the soldiers' boots and guns, the green
tanks on the streets, the silence and hunger of those who turned
away from love, ignored the strangled, limp bodies beaten blue,

thrown into the river, stacked along walls inside the camps.
The coup was also seven years that summer. Still its ash rained
through the city, a blanket of gray soot. It clung to the crevices
of all hearts, latched itself to every muscle. Every day, I cradled
my bird, its hollow bones, pulled it close to my chest, inhaled
its musk and waited for song and spell to wake us into living.
I waited for hours, crushing my bird with hope.

III.

I sat in the birdcage every day the summer before we left
Santiago, stared at all the birds. Their delicate bodies
and wings knew nothing of my sadness. Abuela promised
to keep my bird, to watch it while we flew to a flat land
with white snow in January. One morning, the light still
low and slight along the horizon, I forgot to latch the door.
The birds danced out into the sky. The cage suddenly empty,
its door a sad tongue hanging open. Abuela left fruit and seed,
hoping to lure birds back. Weeks passed. We often heard
their singing near as the sun fell through the horizon.
They never came back. We left in March. It has
been decades. I never returned to the birdcage.
Now I look for birds with claws, beaks that kill.

Immigration Office, Oklahoma City, Oklahoma, 1985

Stowaway, I asked, reading
the options on the sweat-stained
form he held out,
his eyes quiet and begging.
You came by water?

My father wore his only suit that day,
white shirt, knit tie, the smell
of dry cleaning still stuck
inside the blue, pilling wool.
Not a man for words or mercy,
caught between anger and disgust,
my father stared forward,
hands folded tightly over
a manila envelope, ignored
my attempts, meek and uncertain,
to help the man pressing paper
in front of me.

I was a child, ten or eleven, sitting
in a hard, plastic orange chair
in the buzz of fluorescent lights,
mosquitoes looking for blood
in a windowless room
roped off by country of origin.
Bodies grew limp, eyes grew small
staring at the empty, stale walls.
Our forms filled out in English.
Our number forty-three.
We waited for time to move.

I never asked his name, guessed only
that he needed words on paper
with something about the truth

in some kind of English.
I knew nothing of hiding,
the steel guts of boats on water,
legs and arms cramped and crammed,
whispers in fear, cold nights riding
inside a metal shell along
an ocean and no compass,
hoping for another daylight.

My family traveled by passport,
stamped documents,
signatures signaling we
belonged, even with immigrant names,
immigrant forms, immigrant fears.
We were just hopeful, just hungry,
just poor enough to believe we were safe
in secondhand clothes, broken, polite English,
Spanish whispered only at night,
surrounded by cowboys, cattle, and oil.

At the time, it could not strike me,
the category "stowaway,"
or that its reality lived with
this man and his desperate eyes. I only
knew one ritual of immigration,
the waiting rooms, the forms, the disdain
of officers behind glass
rustling papers, looking for mistakes.

We were a sign of something
still buried but pulsing outward
from Oklahoma to Texas to other
borders, legal, illegal, the things
that happened in between.

We were a sign, but I knew
from the eyes, the rough grain
of his hands, the soft *por favor*,
the urgent fear of the alien,
he was not like us.

What Remains Buried

The CIA's plan to disrupt Salvador Allende's candidacy in Chile was called Track I. As time went on, Track I expanded to encompass a wide range of political, diplomatic, psychological, and economic policies, as well as covert operations designed to bring about the conditions that would encourage Chileans to stage a coup.
—Machinations in Chile in 1970 (CIA's website)

We buried the silverware on a Sunday
afternoon behind the rose bushes, in deep sand
and gravel imported from Tata's factory.
An army of hands and legs, we hid
in the kitchen, a lookout at the door.
The rest of us carried fistfuls of coffee spoons,
forks, butter knives, across the terrace. We snaked
through wicker furniture, bare feet on red clay,
ran to the far corner of the backyard, scooped out
mounds of dirt, digging out wet heaps with
soup ladles. Five, six, seven, eight holes carved
out of the earth. We threw the silver stash in,
Abuela's wedding dowry, patted down the sand,
laughed about empty drawers cleaned out of utensils,
lonely, friendless spaces, left abandoned.

A coup climate exists within Chile.

Sons, fathers, husbands, executioners. They threw
limp bodies, drugged, broken, out of planes over
the ocean. They buried bodies in the desert.
Starved, beaten, cooked through, electrocuted.
They wanted water and dirt to swallow dissidence,
hide the screams, cover over the blood and spit,
the cracked bones. Colonia Dignidad, Tres Alamos,
Villa Grimaldi, Londres 38, Azola. From Arica
to Chillán they fed death to water, earth, and sky.
Fed bile and spit and sadness to dry, muted places.
Decades later the water graves cannot be found.

Birds peck, scavenge, fly over nameless mounds.
Creatures of flight and song, birds know nothing
of the death flights or the mounds. They witness
only the rain, the buds and flowering plants
that wake with water and light.

It's that son of a bitch Allende.
We're going to smash him.

We wanted to be pirates, a gang. The oldest,
I was seven, maybe, leader to my younger cousins.
We were bored. The sun was out. It was spring.
Our parents were at the dining room table,
lingering over wine, coffee, dessert. Somewhere
laundry spinning. The afternoon breeze filtered
through the windows. We marched past
with kitchen treasures. Something to put into
the ground, something hidden. A world made
of games and sticky candy.

The key is psychological war within Chile.

The truth discovered, our parents marched
to the sand in silence. Forced us to bend
into the dark dirt, watched us scoop, shovel.
Piles and piles of gravel and dirt, mounds
with no evidence inside. We found very little,
a fork, a butter knife. It had all gone missing.
How to discipline the wildness. To find the trail,
the secret passage to the silver. They searched
for weeks, looking through the dirt for signs,
hoped the earth would reveal the order we
ignored. We buried silver, wanting joy in the dirt,
looking for secrets and love in the wet clay.

You have asked us to provoke chaos in Chile.

We did not know the secrets of the ground,
the thick tears absorbed in dank, hidden rooms.
We made funeral pyres out of silver and soil,
little knowing of the pyres to be unearthed,
the dirt and sorrow left to be discovered.
Decades later, we grow our own gardens,
plant our own flower beds, make our own
families and stories. Some of us hide from
the dead of those years, from their bones,
from their longing, their graves, still abandoned.

Ode to My Hair

It was dark, wild, coarse brown-red curls.
It hung, a long thick rope behind me.
A way to hide. A way to be seen. I pinned
or braided it in summer. It was not a crown
but it sparkled, made my whole self feel whole.
This rope a talisman I clung to when I ached
for signs of beauty in the mirror, though I never lived
as if beautiful. No dark forest queen ever envied
my face, eyes, lips, skin, voice. Still, she might
have given a kingdom for my hair, raged through
fire, ravaged whole fields with ice to have it.
My one spark of Venus. Then, one day, months into chemo,
it was gone. It fell out at night in clusters, on the brush in
sad globs and dead clumps, like bits of wood, burned, ashen,
like abandoned gray ghouls left behind after battle.
There was no stopping it. All locks vanished, no more
waves of color and curl. Bare, empty like a field without
poppies. I had nothing to cling to but a strange, bright scalp.
A year later, new growth. New kinks and swirls,
like small sprites. New spirals hang, dangle like crystals
below my shoulders, glowing. Strangers on the street
ask, *Is it real?* No way to hide. Chemicals made me
otherworldly. Coils of slate blue, gray, purple
mixed with white. Alchemy of medicine and time.

The Spell

I think about the smell of bread and sopaipillas,
the morning fog coating the sky. The buildings
gleaming beneath the Andes. It is early, the color
of the night clings to cement streets, the air
cold, bitter. The dawn enters through windows,
underneath doors, the gossamer of waterdrops
and spider webs. In this light, I am still a child,
still hidden beneath knitted blankets, still living
in Spanish, surrounded by family. A time of stories.
But, the shadow is there. A snake waking slowly.
It knows its prey lives in every corner. Before
migration, before life in other languages,
before memories got lost in the seven thousand miles
between Santiago and the Midwest, the story
of the coup claimed my memories, marked all stories,
marked all light. Fed the snow in the mountains,
the screams in the stadium. Fed all life with the secrets
of the missing. It lingered, a fierce companion.
It kept its promise. Thirty years later, I am
its daughter, writing about a past that does not
belong to me, but only belongs to me when
the callampas looked like silk, the color of a silver-blue
ocean, when I walked past shanty towns on my way
to school. Draping clotheslines strung across makeshift
dirt roads. Even then, I knew there was hunger
inside. The thin, metal houses sprung up like
mushrooms after a rainfall. The week before, there
had been nothing. This was the coup. These were
years of silence, my childhood years. Tanks,
soldiers snaked around the city, a machine
of violence and sadness. There was no Chicago boys'
miracle. The blood in the river was blood. The hunger
creeping through the city was hunger. The disappeared
taken in black vans were taken. Their bodies not just

a story. This is the living I did not live, but this is
the past I remember, the living I dream at night.
The whispers, low voices, the fear of dusk closing in,
men, women hiding in building archways, running from
guns and boots, fighting curfews with rocks, glass bottles,
with pain, running home to families restless, waiting.
Running, fighting, bleeding, dying, we all did some
in those years of hunger. Did I? I was barely a girl.
This is the great divide in the tangle, the snarl of memory.
I am hostage to the stories. The people who bled
or screamed or ran, they are at the bottom of the Pacific,
hidden in coliseum walls, forgotten. Exiled fathers,
sisters, lovers. I have not found them but as a song,
a wailing tune, a funeral march, charred bone and dust.
Pulp eulogy, this spell of history, a dingy, broken memory.

Alien Magic

At nine I was certain about Santa Claus.
The oldest, my philosophy was anchored in
our poverty. We lived in church hand-me-downs
delivered in creased brown paper bags.
Hunger never really happened,
but we ate on food stamps, free lunch tickets.
Santa Claus was as real as anything on my lunch tray.
There were too many variables not to believe.

It always began in December on the bus.
After-school debates among those of us living
in married-student housing. Mostly it was
between the Venezuelans and the Ethiopians,
but as the oldest I moderated gestures, facts,
evidence. We struggled with the science of it,
offering theories of flight, the significance
of chimneys, how the man in red ate all the cookies.

When words got lost to our other languages,
we made up for it in volume and voice.
On stoops, we argued for the number of reindeer,
the sled's journey across the equinox. We debated
how Nigeria, Canada, India, El Salvador,
and Iran could all have the same visit
from one man on one night.

We were gangly and strange, living in the flat
lands of the Oklahoma panhandle surrounded
by oil pumps, steer, and cowboys.
Most of us were there for a few years as fathers
worked in labs, in classrooms. Some of us
were exiled. Some of us had visas. Some of us
had no papers at all. Some of us would never
return to the places we dreamed about at night.

We struggled to believe in a mystery that was
not simply the sadness of immigration. The miles
between continents, the distances to our other lands
were insurmountable without the possibility of magic.
Santa Claus was an immigrant necessity, alien like us.
We needed the alien to be magic.

La Doncella

Only beautiful, healthy, physically perfect children were sacrificed, and it was an honor to be chosen. According to Inca beliefs, the children did not die, but joined their ancestors and watched over their villages from the mountaintops like angels.
—The *New York Times*

She would have been like burnt amber,
a skinny oak trunk, spots of black and gray,
smooth like steel, quiet, a girl without sound.

They would have picked her out, chosen
her symmetrical face, pale gray eyes wide
like the ocean she never saw, but dreamt

about in the cold. They would have picked her,
studied her thin hands, her black hair, the way
her legs swung behind her. They would have

told her she was more than a girl. They would
have prayed to find her, known the gods were happy
to love her, taken her from the village with

the other chosen children, cherished young boys
and girls, also beautiful and hungry. They would
have prayed, sung to the gods. They would have

fed them milk, taken them to the stone altar,
the one in the center, looking to the mountains,
toward the ice. They would have prayed until

it was time for the walk. Miles, miles they would
have walked from Cuzco to the summit,
the walk of the children, their priests, the holy

walking children, cold and alone, holding hands,
drinking the calming beer, eating the coca leaves,
wishing for their mothers. A hike to the mountain,

to the gods, the ones who whispered to the priests
that they were the ones to bring and feed and love.
She would have been fifteen. She would have

been small, like a whisper in the snow.
She would have worn the shawl her mother
made her, stained red like the love she left behind.

She would have helped the others, held them to her,
sung the songs and stories. She would have been old
enough to know. She would have hidden it from

the others. She would have done it all on her own
if they let the others rest. She would have done it
for them, so they could remember something more

in the stories, the ones the gods gave them, the ones
about this mountain, this sky. She would do it all.
She would have done it completely, let the frozen

air carry her over to the side of her other life.
She would have done it alone. She would have
done it without a sound, if they let her.

Before Intersectionality

After school, you hid in the bathroom
examining the day's insults
stuck to your face. You punched
lockers. You slammed bedroom
doors. I tried books. I tried invisibility. We
lived our sadness through each other. We
lived our silence too. We straddled
emptiness. Spanish in whispers,
our parents' accents, their fears.
South Carolina, 1986. We were lost
between stories. What could
we choose but silence.

Bird Girl

Half her life, she has been gone in silence. In silence, in the darkness, who took her, who disappeared this girl willowy and sweet? A black bird of a girl with dark liquid eyes, smoke eyes, smoke mouth, a smile like a song, a secret, a smile like light through the leaves of a tree. This girl bird girl laughing girl with no freckles, no moles, just a scar, the scar on her nose, a sliver of a scar, this girl with eyes like rain, silver eyes, silver scar. This bird of a girl with morning ahead of her that day and work and coffee, cream and sugar and coffee, the sun warm on her skin, this bright bird of a girl leaving home for work for school for life. This bird girl who walked from the mall to the beach to the sunset to the rocks after work after school after home she walked and left no prints no scratches no blood no books no pictures no phone just the shadow of herself. Bird girl, who took you bird girl who made you so small we could not find you with any words or guns or people or stories or secrets or love, who made you so small.

To the Boys Who Bully My Nephew in Sixth Grade

Here, take this apple, small and sweet
like the middle of his heart when he was
born, a heart that was not certain how to
beat. Small sack of veins and rice paper–thin
skin, he looked like an old man with wide
gray eyes and wrinkled, newborn bamboo
fingers. Oh, he was a sack of joy then, like
apples in the middle of a pie. Don't get me
wrong, he is now so annoying like the wild
woodpecker that throws his head into
a tree, all day all day all day, a mad mad bird
who beats the same beat with the same
charcoal beak and what you want to say
is, ya, ya, enough hijo, no more banging.

Yes, I know this language of eye rolling.
This wish to stop the sounds from his mouth,
hold his body down, force his mind,
his thoughts, his lanky self to stop, to stop
to be still. Basta, you want to say. No mas.
I know. I have done it. I know this wish.
The wish to freeze time when he throws
his whole body into my arms, like a wilding
thing that cannot feel anger or fear, a boy
who wants to share his blood and the mess
of his mind with you so much he hurts
you in the flight between his body and yours.
He is something like lightning. Or Hermes
mid-run looking for invisible fairies just to
prove they are in the forest. Es mucho, we
say at family dinners, es mucho.

So maybe you see his flutterings, his deep
deep laugh, his body like electricity and you
think, maricón. You think the ugliness of
stale, bare thoughts. Or maybe you are
in the middle of your own wilding and you
wish for love even when your body vibrates.
I do not know. No lo sé. But I know this:
my boy, this strange creature of teeth and heat,
he will outlive me. He will outlive you.
He will outlive even the sun in the sky.

My English Decades

I hear them bellowing, aching across the rumble
of engines, across iron and steel. I hear them
walking the dog on the hard snow
as it glistens, a dying carpet
of bursting stars.

These sounds are like a call to prayers, a sacred, haunted ringing, a bell,
a chant, the last notes of a eulogy. The beating pulse of English, a restless drum,
a dance floor on a Friday night arching to the certainty of shoes and song,
the stomping of lovers' feet. Blood sounds, this ballad, this English
that scares away all ghosts, all doubt, all other sounds. There is
no escape. These are my English decades. They explode across
every corridor of my heart, beating, echoing rhythms of all
days and nights and days again. Still, I am waiting for
other cadences, living in muffled longing,
remembering the guttural churn
of the ocean, the waves of summer
water in January, wishing for
the metal of another city,
a different drum.

In that distant country I hear my grandfather. His body moves
to the murmur of waves and salt. He pulls up crabs
with giant pincers. He is a song before English.
When waking is not waking, there is memory,
my shadow life on the water. I am seven.
I wear an orange sundress and white
sandals, my mouth sticky
with street candy
and Spanish.
I am still
new.

Memory Spaces
—A PechaKucha after Doris Salcedo

[A FLOR DE PIEL]

Even love finds room in
the dark blood box. It rises slowly.
Spreads like water, ocean waves. Keeps time,
keeps memory. Coats the days, the weeks,
the years. Offers resurrection, the promise
for tomorrow. In basement cells, prisoners
held hands, leaning into each other
back to back. Their skin rice paper–thin,
split, wounded, bruised tender.

[ATRABILIARIOS]

Bullet holes still mark buildings
across from La Moneda. Traces
of tanks and boots left behind
and lonely. Shadow feet, gutted and hollow
march, haunting the cobble stone.
They took Allende's body from the side
gate, a door like a mouth, a secret.
He still had shined shoes, despite
the hole in his head.

[UNTITLED (2014)] (Lonely chairs)

After the bombs exploded, there were
parts left behind, a heart, a broken window,
shattered hands and bones. Empty rooms
with blank paper, half-typed, phones ringing
with no answer. They moved right in the same
evening, announced that a new world was coming,
gleaming, vivid, like white walls freshly painted.
They took over the rooms where the ghosts settled.

What remains are the corner places, empty,
made of wood before it splits or burns.

[DESMEMBRADO]

Villa Grimaldi has a daughter's story.
Abandoned, she roamed underneath
the Ombú tree in a thin, green coat.
Her parents watched her from the tower,
naked, slowly taken apart. No voices left
to put her to sleep. She disappeared.

[Noviembre 6 y 7]

I have read testimonios. They spill out
into memory. El Estadio Nacional, a camp
September 11 to November 7, 1973.
Thousands taken. Mothers, wives, daughters
standing beyond the gates, standing, en luto.
They gave bus fare to the ones they let go.
Everyone half-broken, waiting for life, again.

[UNTITLED] (Sheets stacked or maybe fabric)

When they took over the desks and telephones,
the rooms, the doors, all the buildings and all
the hearts inside, they also took the words left behind.
And the voices. Wiped cement dust, the fractured
window shards. Ordered it all. Even the broken
bones. All in a row. Like stacks of paper.
Useless, lonely, like stray socks.

[UNTITLED (1999)] (Red Rose Wall)

The Mapocho river carried bodies
from twilight deaths to the mornings
after curfew. Then they sat in water.
Few recovered. So many only live now
to find, to bury their beloved with roses.
How could it be that in gardens all over
the city, roses still grow.

[PLEGARÍA MUDA]

In an Episcopal Church I say the Our Father
in English. Never the last lines, for thine is
the kingdom and the power and the glory
now and forever. There are priests who said
it was his will to break bones, use wires
and water, hoods and sacks. They believed
in hard wood. They believed in hard stones.
They believed in blood. Decades pass.
God has still not spoken, one way or the other.

[UNTITLED] (Tables, wedged)

We never asked why we could not speak
Spanish. We just didn't. Even if it was stuck,
a wedge in our throats, a piece of our planet left
behind, secret, not wanted. At the dinner table,
there was a secret universe, like galaxies that shine
and flicker to get attention. We let the whole world
grow gray, rather than love in the colors of the past.
Secret. Shameful, that tangle of vowels and accents.

[LA CASA VIUDA]

My mother is silent about those years.
I cannot ask my father. Even though
they both loved together, he left my mother.
Now, she imagines a widow life. Blank walls,
her heart waiting for color. She sits near
the window but no light finds her. The darkness
is inside. I wonder if she carried the curfews
and bullets with her across continents. Her memories
are mute about the decades of sadness.

[SHIBBOLETH]

In the work camps in the north,
they carved white and black stones
with nails and burnt wood. Birds,
crosses, flowers, talismans of waiting
and suffering. Prisoners begged for
the stones to be shipped to wives, mothers,
children who lived shadow lives, wishing
for cracks in the stones to sprout hope.
The guards wanted souvenirs.

[UNTITLED (2007)] (Mirror box)

I see my mother in the mirror, mostly in
the morning. She is there, suddenly,
while I spit toothpaste into the sink.
It is not memory. It is not distant. The wood
nut shade of her hair, her eyes, the sadness
of cracked things, branches, stone, bird eggs
part of her smile. I see that breaking
in my own mouth.

[ATRABILIARIOS]

The planes that flew over La Moneda
were military planes. Dropped bombs,
like sacks of flour and salt that shattered
through walls. Nothing of the earth grew
that day. No growing vines, no green roots,
no grain for bread, all metal, steel, bright.
I wonder about the paper, the chairs,
typewriters and phones. Lonely leftovers,
forgotten like trees in a fire.
There was no wood that day.

[ACCIÓN DE DUELO]

Sometimes fire brings more than
suffering. The phoenix bursts through
its own ash, a miracle of feathers and color.
The women in the squares, those mothers
who wear their luto clothing even now
decades after, they still hope for the bird
to fly out of the fire, out of the wax of
stale candles left lit across the fields of
their memories. They want to see life
burn out of sadness and be life, again.
Whole bodies suddenly rise out of the
square they walk in every Monday
carrying black and white pictures
of their beloved, lost in water, without
any fire to bring them home, keep them
warm, make new feathers and color.

[UNTITLED (2008)] (Paper doors)

My Abuela kept mothballs in her nightstand.
She wanted to keep the creatures out of the wool,
make them wish for other doors and drawers.
Or the moonlight or terrace light.
Not the sweaters made in summer she kept
folded in white paper on the shelves
of her secret world. I never looked inside
any of her boxes. Even as a girl, I waited
for the miracles of yarn to be magic,
like the moths she kept alive at a distance.

[INSTALLATION AT THE ISTANBUL BIENNIAL]
(Hole full of chairs)

In my Tata's factory he made things
out of wood, doors for homes, hotels,
banks. First, he and his father, then his
sons, but not my father who wanted to be
a mathematician. The wood was auburn,
with a thin grain, fuerte he would say,
like teeth. He did not make chairs.
I never asked him why. But I think now
it must be because an orphaned chair is
like a bird missing its wings. It cannot fly.
It cannot dive. It cannot live, this wingless
bird. Just like the chair that has been
abandoned. Widowed. Left to break
on its own.

[UNTITLED] (Cement chair and spikes)

In the interrogations, the guards
and doctors tied the prisoners to a chair
with wire and rope. Loosely. The body
sat taut, wet with blood, tears, urine.
Hands behind, eyes blindfolded, even
though the room was dark. Except for
the light hanging above, a metronome
swinging back and forth, a prayer
with no answer.

[EXPOSICIÓN]

Some prisoners were taken by doctors,
guards with guns pointing. A vaccine they
said. They were being taken to another
camp. Infections could be dangerous.
The ones left behind wearing old clothes
understood, the ones who left would not
come back. But no one knew what happened.
There were stained records found later,
half-filled reports. Witnesses describe the lockers
in the bathroom of the airplane hangar,
sad metal doors left agape. Clothes hanging.
And shoes. All the abandoned shoes,
the ones most of them were wearing when taken
from home, hooded. The ones they walked
to the metro with, went to the candy store in
after work to buy flowers, marzipan for dessert.
When the prisoners who were left were driven
to a different camp, the shoes remained
in lockers, untied.

[UNTITLED] (Rib doors, or bone)

The bed frames were perfect metal
conduits for electricity. Like a cage but
not made of bone. There in the dark,
the guards strapped each body to them
let the car battery do its spark dance. Rattle
teeth and cranium, sometimes ribs cracked
from the jerking. Bodies were held together
after by the sheer power of bones, even if
crushed. In the cells, leaning into each other,
into the walls, the men sang songs
to the broken bits and memories.

[LA CASA VIUDA]

They do not think they are widows.
Black is not the color of death.
It is the color of questions. The color of witness.
Mothers and wives and daughters,
they drink coffee, read mail, water the garden,
feed the dog. They answer the door every day.
They never leave doors unopened.
They open all, looking, asking, wailing.
They wait, still, every day. Threshold
of hope and mourning. They remember
how the beloved looked that night,
dragged out, men and guns pushing through
the bedroom door. They ran to the front
door in their robes, the door of their hearts
breaking in half, split like wood in a drought.

Waiting for the Horsemen

To Document

To mark, to list, to catalogue, to register, to chronicle, to cite, to make, to seal, to stamp.

We think in ceremonies of paper. We document in straight, sharp lines. Imagine charts reveal stars and sky, black holes. As if charts reveal the galaxy. As if the universe hangs on a wall. As if time lives in rigid, measured lists. We cling to ledgers. Sad ink moments. Dead-eye accounting, these rules of the law. Paper means nothing.

Who is real. Who is allowed. Who is loved. Who is ours.

When You Go Out to Walk the Dog

You call me at 10:14 p.m. I think:
He has been kidnapped or shot or maybe
it is aliens or wild dogs. Someone is dead or
he lost his shoe in a sinkhole. The dog
is rabid, or maybe the dog is the dead one.
Come outside, you laugh. You are
standing on the lawn holding
a bag of shit and the dog leash. You say
look, look at the moon. And I do.

In the Time of the Patriarch

For Aimee

The boots march in step. Armies of sadness each day
a day closer. All seems to stop but the time of the patriarch.

Cancer cells grow like strange vines, bouquets in blood,
swimming in black lanes like pinballs in a maze.

Turkey vultures cut through bullet-steel skies with finger
wings, looking for possum carcasses and squirrel heads.

Butterflies lost at sea, thrown off track by gusts,
pulse their battered wings in aimless circles.

In the meantime: we will cling to the world of light,
look to the sun, talisman, sign of the ancestors.

We will birth our bodies out of sky dust and heat,
constellations bursting out through black holes.

We will sprout song out of our mouths, crucibles
of joy sounding out the blood ways of our stories.

We will become myth, Medusa, Cleopatra, Guadalupe,
inhabit mitochondrial time, live out of fire and breath.

Machines and madness tell only the end of time.
We will tell the time of mothers and daughters.

We will keep the time of love.

Villa Grimaldi

Tongue-red gate. Steel mouth opens
to a speckled cement sidewalk. No blood now.
No broken bits of teeth and buttons.

The hanging tree in the middle. Lotus flower shape.
Sky catcher. Once upon a time a body rack.
Heavy sacks swinging. Legs, arms, gasps, part the wood.

Beyond the Ombú a rose garden. Memory space.
Thick reds, yellows. Names in calligraphy on wooden plates.
Hundreds. Buried with each bush.

At the edge of the park, empty mermaid-green tiled
swimming pool. Brown granite mural. Lists of the Missing.
Coarse crabgrass bursting out

beyond the stone walls, the Andes,
snow torches, looming.

What It Takes

It is going to take bodies, it always does.
This world that eats fire and drains spirit,
it takes bodies to push up the sun, to make
birds fly, to plant flowers and make bread.
It takes bodies to make blood move.
There is nothing without the bodies.

Bodies speak the scars. Bodies carry
the world and the weight of sorrow
and song. It takes so many voices,
millions of sounding voices in the sky,
in the water, in the dirt, to ring, to rise
to breathe song into the silence.

There are others, to be sure. Puppets who
speak with serrated tongues about order,
law, respect. They want to hide their hearts
in the sand. Stay sleeping, in wait for a prince,
or a dwarf maybe, at least some others,
some other eyes and hands and hearts
to do the suffering, do the breaking.

Silly birds. All bodies die in a drought.

Forerunner

> He was not that Light but was sent to bear witness of that Light.
> —Gospel of John, 1:8

John ate locusts, wandered
around, spent time restless,

no blind men to cure. An angel
declared his birth a first act, a herald

of sorts, I suppose. He wore camel
hair shirts, muttered to the wind

about his cousin and miracle water.
He followed the rules by all accounts

with little drama. Spent days in
dry dirt with bugs and honey.

Luke says they flocked to him,
or is it Peter? He put on a show.

Baptize with muddy water, a bit
of wet spit. Hustled the crowds,

promising a future while they
waited on the headliner.

Did he know about betrayal? How
it would end? Did he care, ask

for a pass, a way out? Did he beg
for a reprieve far from dancers,

silver trays, and kings? Jesus is easy.
Witnesses wrote every word,

Waiting for the Horsemen

We wake up in a world sharp, angular with blades ready
for blood. This machine world is not made for light.
Only steel words. Sanguine words, ready for cutting, slicing,
gutting. Ready for bones. No arias sprout from mouths.
Our mouths are sewn shut, one stitch at a time, like buttonholes
sealed with fishing string. No warm sand to stand in.
This world hard and dry, made of boots and tanks and edicts.
No love songs flutter, no birds find sky, no shores spring life.
We live in the desert, waiting, as madmen and armies advance.
Marching, blighting the sun, shooting out the stars for sport.
There are no words like *love*, like *forgive*, like *yes*. There are
only bricks. There are only charred hearts. There are only
wrecked bits of bodies and soot. Our tongues have been split.
We can only swallow blood. We can only wait for the horsemen.

What You Are Doing Is Living

It is deep growing. Your body the culprit. It spreads.
Not like water or the sun across a sharp, blue sky.

It is more the mush of crabs after the tide has come and gone,
leaving its ravages on the beach to ache against the heat

drying up the wet bodies into pulp. Too much life. That is
what the doctor says. Many routes of muscles, blood

to dance with, invade. So many ways to make mountains
of death. There are marks. Afterthoughts. Stretch of color.

Strangeness. Messages to find if you are paying attention.
Not that you usually do. The symbols are hard to read.

Crawl around silent. You have no time for the bombs stuck
inside the guts of things. Your bones. Your heart. Your liver.

Why look for the marrow. So much to look for in living.
Or so you thought. You really cannot be prepared.

The phone calls, the tests, the blood you watch creep out
into plastic vials. There are so many of these moments

you forget what you are doing is living.

Flight

Ladies and gentlemen, welcome aboard.
Please pay attention to the following safety announcement.

This plane is equipped with six exit doors, two over the wings,
two at the front, and two at the back of the plane. Take a moment
to locate the exit closest to you. Note that the nearest exit may be behind you.

Remember the exits in case you suddenly realize
there is no way you can stay on the plane. It might
be easier to leap into the blue and white than face
the onslaught of your in-laws, their sour stares
waiting for you just beyond the gate. You might be
better off not arriving. Enjoy instead the prospect
of escaping their bird jabs about your work,
your childless womb and choices. The cabin doors
midair a welcome chance to land somewhere,
anywhere else, even if the jump kills you.

In the event of a loss of cabin pressure, oxygen masks will deploy
from above your seat. Place the mask over your mouth and nose.
Be sure to secure your own mask before helping others and children.

If you left your child with your husband, your mother
to take a completely useless trip for work, try not
to think about her. Crazy, wild girl who runs around
the house in her underwear, a wand, a Halloween wig
from two years ago, though it is the dead of winter.
If you managed to convince yourself, your mother,
you did not want children, remember you believe it,
still. Put the mask on safely, knowing you leave no
one person attached to you for those early months
of sleepless love. Tell yourself you have other joys.

Though the bag may not inflate, be assured oxygen is flowing through it.

Flowing like sadness at the thought of not seeing
your niece again. She has no idea your mind traveled
to her at this moment thirty-five thousand miles above
the ocean. Or to the summer you taught her to fish, play
hopscotch outside behind the garage. She stained herself
with chalk all week. Every dress, every T-shirt marked
with dusky pink-blue pastel handprints. Unabashedly
she asked for ice cream dinners every night, spit out all
the broccoli you steamed. She made you laugh despite
the waste. She made you love dirty clothes and mops.

If there is a loss of cabin lighting, floor lights will illuminate
a path to the nearest exit.

This plan for illumination is not likely to bring much
clarity about your writing, the empty pages you leave
behind, pages you tried to ink up but failed every day
to write. Instead you managed the chaos: laundry, taxes,
the grocery store, the pharmacy, the farmer's market,
the kids' sleepovers, summer camps. The floor lights
will not lead you to the words left undiscovered,
the words gone missing. The tangled syllables
of your father's silence. Secrets like underground roots.
Love. Forgive. Grace. Lingering vines, never planted.

In case of a water landing, your seat cushion is an approved
flotation device. Simply remove the seat and hold it tight
across your chest.

Ignore the tightness in your chest. Anger, anxiety,
the thought of plunging into water, an empty dark
desert without having taken a moment to look at

your husband before you crawled out of bed. Avoid
thinking about the five minutes you wanted to hold him
but did not. Feel the deep rhythm of his breathing,
the way his mouth stays slightly open when he sleeps,
the way his hair shoots up from the pillow, how he
smells like wood, soap. His body the promise of your days,
your nights. His body a furnace no matter what season.

Life vests are located beneath your seats. Simply pull them
over your head and walk to the nearest exit. Do not inflate
your vest until after you have exited the plane. The beacon light
will automatically flash once you are in the water.

It will not be the ocean of your childhood, the Pacific,
so cold, so biting it burned your bones with cold even
in summer. You were a fish, a mermaid, brown and freckled,
making pets of crabs and starfish, killing them every
week with your love, but every week trying again.
Your grandfather warned you they needed the salt,
seaweed to survive. He never stopped you. Let you torture
those sad creatures. How little you knew of loss, of leaving
never to return to that time and those years. He would
die the year after you left that small country behind.

The captain has turned off the "fasten seat belt" sign. You are
free to move about the cabin, but as rough air can happen
suddenly, please keep your seat belts secured tightly across
your waist when you are seated.

When you feel the clasp of the fabric and metal around you,
you sense the turbulence. The plane defies gravity, stays in
the sky, mocking you with promised death, real and coming,
if not today. Looking out the oval window, you recall your days,
months and years wasted in worry, a sad poison, like a river

snake roped around your heart. Envy, guilt, regret, muses
of dirt and sadness shackled you to small, cement wonders.
Suspended thirty-five thousand feet above your life, the plane
reminds you of death in every cell. You become a prisoner
of metal and steel regret. In living, you erased the sky.

Why is it on the ground, you forget the lesson of flying?

I Was a Bell

Pacific Dreams

How long since my body
carried joy? Since my hands,
my legs plunged into the cold
ache of the Pacific? How long
since my bones felt the bite
of the water, its sting of sand
and seaweed? Strange, dream
ocean. It leaves me breathless,
this memory. Eyes closed, head
submerged beneath the waves,
dark cocoon of foam and salt
engulfing everything. Beneath
the waves, my body a muffled,
quivering heartbeat.

Rebellion

My grandmother asked if I would ever have
a garden. By then, her body pulsed, pumped
rabid cells. Her skin radiated yellow, the color
of dying lights, nothing like the color of her
roses when I was a child. She did not wear gloves
to sculpt the flowers in the front yard. Even in
winter, she lifted out life, one mound at a time.

In the time of Pinochet, the flowers grew under
her hands. They clung to her voice. Prayers for
children, a son, a daughter forced into leaving.
They wanted joy, rejected the General's torture
machines invading the ocean, the vineyards,
the mountains. Left behind, she pruned in silence,
planted flowers of rebellion, waited for the fall.

When I landed decades later, she had not seen
her garden in years, its thick, delicate vines
the color of coffee, strung together with twine.
The head of each rose a hat, some timid, slight,
others anxious shades still waiting for water,
for sun. She loved them with blades and blood,
spent her days coaxing them into colors.

Then, I lied about having a garden. In her bed, she
looked so small, the yellow-green of dry, withered ferns.
I would have a garden somewhere in the hills
of a state she never knew, could not pronounce,
would never visit, could not find on a map.
But she willed it into being those thirty years before,
when she planted my return.

The Generals of South America

Why is it that when I look at the dictators of South America
I see my grandfather, *El Turco* as they called him,
creased, weathered skin, teeth and mouth ready to smile.
I see these generals of Chile or Argentina or Cuba, and in Fidel
I see my father, Old World, black-bearded, thin-faced,
ready for prayers, for oaths, for Sunday lunch with wine.
These are pictures of men I know. On CNN they tell me
about their dirty wars, their missions of disappearing
thousands, using electricity and hoods and dark vans
in the middle of the night, the tentacles of power covering
a whole nation in the darkness of what happens after a coup.
I have read about mangled bodies, blood and vomit on metal
slabs, priests giving benedictions for death squads, for infants
wrestled out of mothers' bodies, stolen and given to señoras
with manicured lawns, pressed pastel suits, and rose gardens.
But I look at these pictures of the Generals of South America
and see men I know and love and miss in death. And I wonder
about the daughters, the ones who sit in courtrooms, and
listen to their fathers' lives of torture and midnight shootings
and electricity in the soft-blue places of the body, and I wonder
if they see their fathers still in those faces.

In the Poison Time There Is Love

They were a cancer, he said. Early summer, after Sunday lunch,
thick heat circling above the patio. There were pisco sours,
olives, cheese, and bread. My younger cousins smoked in silence.
My aunt cleared the table. He sat full and sleepy, a wet drink
sweating in his hand. *Eran un cáncer.* The birds talked. Afternoon
breezes carried their song across the backyard. The flowers
in their clay pots were striking batons of color my aunt carved
out of soil and dirt on weekends. *No tienen vergüenza.* You do not
know that time, he said. *Comunistas. Terroristas en las calles.*
Todo se iba a la mierda. He sipped his cold drink, leaned back
against the chair, a long, thin scowl on his face. *Eran un cáncer.*
Y ese museo es una vergüenza.

My cancer, stage two with lymph node–positive engagement.
The lump bloomed to five centimeters between mammograms.
That November my fingers felt thickness along the breast, a tight
tendon, long muscle strings. Something hiding. Strange, restless
cells. Spiculated. A mass with spokes, a star illuminating beneath
tissue and fat. It was a winter diagnosis. Christmas and cinnamon
scented. Ice and snow growing in the sky. I waited for biopsies,
PET scans, MRIs, CT scans. Tests, blood, tests, blood. I drank
thin, alkaline milkshakes to light up the insides of my chest, liver,
lungs, spine. The fear: shadows on other organs, beyond breast,
beyond lymph nodes, spidering their way across my body.

A year and a half later, no evidence of disease. I spent two months
in Santiago. A celebration trip. In a healed body, I walked paths where
other bodies were broken, burned. Daughters, fathers went missing.
Swimming pools became water graves. Electricity lit the tender parts
of so many lovers. My second week there, I lied to my aunt about my plans.
Took the metro to the memory museum, wandered in aimless sadness.
Londres 38. Another lie. I sat on the second floor staring at white-gray
faded walls. How did no one hear the screams? Villa Grimaldi a week
after that. I walked the park. In the back corner, a thick stone wall

of names. Black and white pictures cover rose garden, murals, sidewalks.
Handwritten signs line the grass. *Dónde están? Dónde están? Dónde están?*
The question of every survivor.

Chemo kills cells flowering inside. Other cells die too. Hair falls
out. Skin grows red with rashes. Forearms and cheeks blister. Mouth
sores sprout. Bones pulse, ache with poison. Counts drop. The liver
rages against the fruit punch–colored cocktails. Days, weeks, months
lost to emptiness and pain. Still, in the poison time there is love.
I was loved. Skin, hands, heart. Beloved. In the chemo room my hands
were warmed, my legs covered with soft cotton blankets. In the cancer
room I was fed. There were no hoods. There were no dank rooms
with secrets and darkness to beat out confessions. In the cancer
room, there was no wondering about dark.

In those years before, those years of silence, whole worlds fell
through the sky on Wednesday death flights. Now, the disappeared
still haunt rivers, deserts, oceans. Linger mashed to bits inside mute,
unmarked mounds, graves where blood seeped slowly out of men,
women, children. What more can be charred? What more can be
consumed? *Eran un cáncer,* he growled. I know cancer. Every mouth
sore, every rash, every fever, every needle, every night sweat,
every moment of blood and pain. Everywhere, there is love.

Someday I Will Visit Hawk Mountain

I will be a real birder and know raptors
by the shape of their wings, the span of them
against wide skies, the browns and grays
of their feathers, the reds and whites like specks
of paint. I will look directly into the sun, point and say,
those are black vultures, those are red-shouldered
hawks. They fly with the thermals, updrafts, barely
moving, glide their bodies along the currents, borrowing
speed from the wind. I will know other raptors,
sharp-shinned hawk, the Cooper's hawk, the ones
that flap their wings and move their bodies during the day.
The merlins, the peregrine falcons, soaring like bullets
through blue steel, cutting the winds looking for rabbits,
groundhogs that will not live past talons and claws.
I will know the size of their bones, the weight
of their beaks. I will remember the curves, the colors
of their oval, yellow eyes. I will have the measurements,
the data that live inside their bodies like a secret
taunting me to find its guts. Or this is what I tell myself.
But, I am a bad birder. I care little about the exact rate
of a northern goshawk's flight speed. I do not need
to know how many pounds of food an American kestrel
eats in winter. I have no interest in the feather types
on a turkey vulture. I have looked up and forgotten
these facts again and again and again. They float
out of my mind immediately. What I remember:
my breathless body as I look into the wildness above,
raptors flying, diving, stooping, bodies of light, talismans,
incantations, dust of the gods. Creatures of myth,
they hang in the sky like questions. They promise
nothing, indifferent to everything but death.
Still, still, I catch myself gasping, neck craned up,
follow the circles they build out of sky, reach
for their brutal mystery, the alien spark of more.

After the Election: A Father Speaks to His Son

He says, they will not take us.
They want the ones who love
another god, the ones whose
joy comes with five prayers and
songs to the sun in the mornings
and at night. He says, they will
not want us. They want the ones
whose tongues stumble over
silent *E*'s, whose voices creak
when a *th* suddenly appears
in the middle of a word.

They want the ones who cannot hide
copper skin like we can. He says,
I am old. I lived through one revolution.
We can hide our skin.
We have read the books.
He says, we are the quiet kind, the ones
who stay late and do not speak,
the ones who do not bring trumpets
or trouble. He says, we are safe in silence.
We must become ghosts.

I think, so many are already dust.
Tried to stay thin, be small, tried
breaking bone and voice, tried
to be soft. So many tried to be
empty, to be barely breath. To be
still enough to be left alone. Become
shadows, trying not to be bodies.

It never works. To become nothing.
They come for the shadows, too.

Immigrant Confession

The Cherokee are not originally from Oklahoma. Settlers forced
them to move west, into air and sky, beyond buildings,
beyond concrete, beyond the rabid land hunger. There was
a trail. There was despair. Reservations carved out of prairie
grass and sadness in the middle of flat dirt. We landed
in March 1980. We knew nothing about the Cherokee.
Settlers from the South, driven by opportunities and education,
looking for the gold and gifts of immigration, we hid our Spanish,
the shame of accents and poverty, immersed ourselves in cowboy
ways. In school we learned English, read about open, endless land,
a territory there by divine right (they said) for those willing,
chosen to till and build, for those broken out of other lands.
Every spring the second grade celebrated the land rush. Half of us
immigrants flung across the globe, we wanted to be part of the story.
We gathered in costume behind the chalk line in a field across from
Westbury elementary. Girls in calico skirts, bonnets, ruffled blouses.
Boys in straw hats, borrowed cowboy boots, chaps strapped with toy guns.
Parents and picnic lunches waited on the sidelines. The cap gun popped.
The second grade scattered free, running, stakes in hand, ready to claim
our piece of promised land. My parents celebrated the land rush twice,
two of us old enough to live into the strange alchemy of assimilation.
I learned later our stakes traded in death, crushed and cut away love
from the arid land with the wave of a flag, the pulsing stampede of wagons,
the firing of the starting gun. So much made missing with every second-grade
spring picnic. Two million acres of territory taken in the first land rush.
My immigrant confession: I have ached for my Oklahoma childhood,
my territory story, when the land gave again, held a promise of country
after migration. I have mourned the second-grade land rush, the look on
my parents' faces as we galloped into yellow grass, screaming breathless
in joy and wildness, when they imagined an America big enough,
wide enough, whole enough to let us in, whole enough not to break us.

I Was a Bell

Diagnosis: Dyspareunia, Female
Alternative: Atrophic Vaginitis

My body. I have

forgotten

my body.

Part I
Round, soft, too big now. I carry it,
a brown, faded sack, half-empty
and dry. An afterthought of muscle
and fat. It was never much, no luminous
skin or bright blood, always a work-machine.
It was always too much and too little. It
was always hungry and full. It was
a drooping flower, or a bush that needed
too much water and light. Still,
it was mine to run with, mine to use.

Dyspareunia is pain that is associated with sexual activity.
This condition ranges from mild to severe.

Part II
You loved all the scars, the extra thick
middle parts. Once, when we were young,
you carried me in the rain, ran five blocks.
Me on your back, puddles
and water and cement all mixed in,
mixed up in the city as you galloped
from the Boylston T to Beacon Street.
We were new to love. Inside
your basement apartment, still wet, still

laughing, still. My skin, freckled
and slick, touched your skin, blue veins
and life holding me, my arms, my legs.

> *This can affect any part of the genitals or lower abdomen,*
> *and there are many possible causes. Depending on the cause,*
> *dyspareunia may get better with treatment, or it may return*
> *(recur) over time.*

Part III
For years in the dark, you held me
and my body. You made wholeness out
of broken things, took the cracked parts,
shards and pieces. You were a musician.
I was a bell. You made my whole throat
sing. I was metal and curves. I was musk
and wood, a tower ringing. I was the water
in the river, the waves in the ocean. I was
the warmth and color of butterfly wings.
My singing years. Decades of sound.
My whole body marked time in music.

> *RISK FACTORS: Certain conditions or situations may lower*
> *a woman's estrogen level, which increases her risk of atrophic vaginitis.*
>
> *These include: Being treated with X-ray treatment (radiation)*
> *or medicines (chemotherapy).*

Part IV
I never wanted children. Alien cells
and tissues leeching, aching for life
inside. Crab creatures, half-starved,
clinging for love. Parasites hanging,
half-baked yeast grabbing at blood

and body, draining all liquids. Demanding,
they have seemed, children. Wreaking
through a life like fire, torching
fauna and field. Combustible. All knees
and hands and eyes begging for more.
More. More. I never wanted children.
But now. This brown sack of mine cannot
even make them. All gone, the warmth
and water, the blood of possibility. No
longer in the singing part of my body.

*CAUSES: The cause of this condition is not always known.
Possible causes include:*

Cancer.

Flight Plan

The Order of Things

As with all things now, I want order.
I want to take the strings of chaos, the
lonely stamp, the leftover paper,
the bruised, too-ripe peach, the thick
flyaway gray hairs and stack them.
Stack them in a row. Put them in a box.
Label each part, taking time to make
sure I note the skin of the peach,
the wire tangle of the hair, the missing
colors on the faded stamp. I want
to make them whole again, full and
not dead or dying. Order is a place
of rest and stopping. Long ago I said
I wanted to be light, the way silk feels
light against the heat of the sun.
I imagined floating in this world, always
sure of how beautiful the mess would be.

But I have learned cells can grow to wild
proportions. Along the inside pulsing parts
of the body, carving their path with serrated
blades along muscle tissue, the pink inside
of the breast. Under the arm, reaching for
the small, jellyfish glands. This was more
than a mess. Those cells, an aching
mouth of angst and blood, urgent for
the rest of it, the rest of me. And I alone
in this jungle of living, a stumbling
wanderer. This is not the story I wanted.

Relics

I put up a tree with ornaments
my mother painted twenty years ago
in a rural Oklahoma town. Just arrived,
she wanted to make relics out of the sadness
of immigration, paint things to pass down,
something to give daughters, something
more than aching and loneliness. A small,
sleeping mouse on a moon, a bronze sleigh
with polka-dot packages, two angels
in blue with bronze trumpets ringing.
These the anchors of our new lives,
the ones lived in the cold, the snow,
in the glaring flatlands with alien
oil machines. I hang my mother's
ornaments, signs of when we lived
in hope of green cards, longed for
a house, avoided Spanish.

His mother dressed him in his middle
school graduation suit. Wool pinstripe,
a yellow tie, a pocket square, worn
leather shoes with leather soles.
Shoes that shimmer black against
the white silk he lies in. She hangs
ornaments on a tree. She will pick out
the cotton ball–bearded popsicle stick
Santa he made in third grade, the one
he still wanted to hang in his lanky
boyhood years. He strutted around
in a T-shirt, black boots, wailing
"Santa Claus Is Coming to Town."
Even at thirteen he put out cookies,
waited for the miracle of the early
morning magic.

Today I plug in my tree.
Today she plugs in a curling
iron to press her hair into curls
that would fit beneath the veil
of her hat with bobby pins. I drink
my wine, listen to music. She sits
in the front row looking. Her son,
all fifteen years of him in a box.
He is quiet, still. There is a crowd
of faces in the church. They are
calm, silent. They are without
words. A minister explains that
the Lord is her shepherd, that he
gives only what she can take.

She will not see her son's wide
smile, his hands, the way they cradle
his dog's head. She will not see
his clothes and books clogging
up the house. She will not see
him at the table after work,
scold him for using the wrong
fork. He will not become
a man. She will not live all
the mysteries of motherhood.

I sit at night in front of my tree,
think of my mother, her fragile
hope mapped onto ornaments
now sitting on the branches,
clay and color illuminated. It is
soft, like the pause in the middle
of the story. Whatever sorrow

lingers, my mother sees daughters
living in a world of light.

There is a mother sitting alone
without a son. Her hope does not
breathe. She does not live in
a world of light. A mother had
a son, a son who grew into the echoes
of manhood. Only some sons grow
beyond dreams. In this world
of broken fire, some mothers live
only to bury bones.

Marriage

At night he listens, not for nightingales
or sirens or dying stars. He listens
for the bedroom door, her dress
rustling as she undresses, her breathing,
the humming in her mouth. He listens
for the faucet, the dresser drawer, the book
pages opening after she turns on
the light on the nightstand. She makes
a song of her whole body, every movement,
the jar of face cream clinking on the sink,
the hairbrush through her hair, the liquids
of her night routine, her half-sung song,
the symphony of her life. He listens
to the secret story, her lonely words,
the sorrow that clings like water
to the walls, a draped shroud of regret.
The bed moves, the light a sliver under
the door. He listens from the hallway.
He sits on the top stair, on the other side
of the door. He knows she is still awake,
imagines the heat of her body under
the covers, volcanic, like charcoal
exploding. She will say nothing when
he slides into the room. She will not speak.
The heat will die before he finishes opening
the door. He will not find love. She will not
find warmth. They will sleep on different
sides. The cold of other planets and stars
will live between them, and the years will
be missiles, armed, ready for war.

Twelve-Hour Shift

My father wore a blue apron,
circled the main floor selling

bingo cards. Did he eat? Did he
sleep? Was his accent too

thick? Twelve-hour shifts, secret
money. My mother claims

to remember nothing. What can it
tell me, this detail of immigration.

Still, I am Frankenstein. Sew
together a lonely heart, a gloomy

mouth, a weary hand. Look for
stories in bits of skin. Suture

mystery and memory. Stare
at the dead.

You Have to Leave Me Twice

She said it as if it were
a casual thing. Split the ashes,
one for the velatorio here, one for
the family mausoleum. Be sure
the bones are dust enough
to fit in a tin can so they do not
give you a hard time at security.
This is the great divide, *mitad*
y mitad. Entiendes? Me repartes.
This is how you bury your dead.
There will always be two places.
Siempre hay dos. The immigrant
always carries twin shadows. *Siempre*
esta la sombra. You cannot choose
North, South, English, Spanish.
You can only split sorrow.
No hay medio, entiendes? The body
has life, but the dead, they have
little weight but sadness. *Así es,*
mijita, así es. You have to travel to live.
You have to travel to die.
Me tienes que dejar dos veces.
You have to leave me twice.
El alma dividida en dos. One soul,
two eternities. She stops.
Then she asks about the dog.

A Love Story

Sometimes I hate my dog for weeks at a time.
She has hind-leg shakes, a white muzzle beard,
rotting incisors. She is twelve, but who really
knows what fur says about age. It still
shimmers in the sunlight, glows beads
of diamond water after thunderstorms.
She does not know moderation, still bolts up
at any sound, the dryer buzzer, a third-floor
goblin, the dishwasher beep, sirens on
the television. A half-hearted watchman,
she opens one eye to growl at the hidden
mysteries of the day. She worships every
corner with sun, body stretched, legs pushed
forward, drapes herself across the light sifting
through any window. She pants feverishly
but does not relent when sun finds its way
into the house. Must be the stubborn grit
of old age, this need, this ferocious need
for light and heat. We agree only on the sun.
She rattles me on most every other point,
the constancy of her presence, her demands,
her compulsion to exist in space, my space,
seep and saturate my existence. She is a strange
vampire pulsing, pulsing, drinking all blood,
all liquids, forcing me to know her when
what I want is to forget. This is the dance
of loving an alien. Or maybe it is the sign
of insanity, this urge to force her out
of my head, out of my heart. Wicked,
she reminds me I am not the center.

Flight Plan

My father challenged
the mystery of flying.
A mathematician, he lived
rooted in the certainty
of Bernoulli and Newton.
He trusted fast-moving air
at lower pressure, believed
in the curvature of wings,
their slight tilt down
to the angle of attack.

It is 5,066
miles from Santiago, Chile
to Oklahoma City, Oklahoma.
Thirty-one, three children,
no English, my mother
whispered her sadness to no one.
She swallowed every heart
beat, stifled all sorrow. It
was March. It was 1980.
The coup was still a bright blue
wound. The plane pulsed
through clouds, miles, memory.

After hours, after questions,
after all stories ended, she
promised angels. One on each
wing lifting the taut, cold
steel body. A plane under
divine command to stay
in the sky. We would land
in oil and cattle country
where my father waited.

It worked, this myth of love,
the comfort of a father holding
up a burning cylinder, a mystery
of girlish faith. I closed my eyes
and slept. The plane crossed
the South, the Midwest, landed
in an arid, yellow prairie of steer
ranches, dirt, casinos. In a new
world of upside-down seasons,
January became winter.

Decades pass and I carry
rosary beads. No certainty with
any sky. No angels, no fathers now.
I left cowboy and cattle country.
I have studied my own physics,
learned my own plane myths.
But every takeoff is still a new
standoff with gravity. I am seven
looking through oval windows,
waiting for divine command.

My Yellow Heart

I remember the yellow
of my childhood,
the first paint after we
moved in. Everything
was vinyl siding and love.

My sisters and I danced
around the house. Tall
ladders, anchored tentacles,
hung along the sides.
We danced a bright, joy dance.
Our first house.
Our only house.

My father stood
on the lawn looking
up, pointing, directing
the painters. He climbed
to the roof, a younger man
still with us, he looked
down, we were
there in the gaze
of his brown eyes,
bright skin, still under
his spell, his promises.

Thirty-five years later
I stand in the doorway.
He is yellow, barely able
to get out of bed. Surgery scars
fresh, bleeding. The bedroom is
all shadows, furniture I do not
recognize. He is his own ghost.
His midlife crisis cracked all spells,

all promises. Still he demands
this daughter pilgrimage.

Strange what time does
to the shape of a father,
the shade of a father. It does
its own demanding. Makes its
own yellow, a dry wreath looping
through a harvest of hearts.
The following spring, he
moved out, sold the house.
I never saw the new color.

Confessions

Chilenos, my parents do not divorce.
They dance around questions of hell and the church
by living two states apart and discussing grandchildren.
My father's last confession was a decade before
Pinochet's soldiers marched into La Moneda
with machine guns and the CIA,
before bodies disappeared through the Mapocho River,
purple, half-naked, and tortured,
before women's pants were sliced open for the General
by armed men, boys really, thrilled
at the prospect of knives and thighs.
When September came, my father stopped
worrying about what happens after death.
Bloodied streets and tanks and boots
kept confession active in other ways.
They came in cement corridors made for football
and evening rodeos. They came with electricity and wires
on soft, intimate parts, the pink of body seams.
Now, my parents never confess, not to me, not to each other.
Catholic, my mother keeps the riddle of those years.
She will not confess immigrant wounds in English.
Estos Americanos will not understand, she tells me, even
the priest, with his tassels and robes still *un gringo*
when it comes to foreign policy. But divorce
is a sin, or something like that,
so, they live separate lives, ignore the law,
confess everything but their sadness.

Cells

Before, there were whole years,
decades of time. I had millions
of feelings and words and
memories. Nothing about white
blood cells. Warm, milky
contrast dyes swimming inside
my torso. Face down in an MRI
tube. An éclair of magnetic sounds.
I still feel the thick, wet liquid
as it creeps through veins, into
my breast. Serpent harbinger.
It is not sweet.

A year. A series of plastic bags.
Neon-red chemo cocktail every
three weeks. My mouth sores
blossomed. My tongue tasted
salt and sandpaper for days
after the bright pulp merged
with blood and fat. Walking
made every bone ring in wild
orange pain. Everywhere
savage cells. Missiles in wait.

How much time escaped out
of my body. I wonder this now,
looking into the hollow heart of it.

Rooted

For Natalia

When I held her a decade and some ago,
she was a world of blood, a slight sack with
wide eyes and a hungry mouth. Small succubus.
Demanding. Angry. Yet beloved, so beloved.
My mother, my father, my sister, we all traveled
three time zones to hold her, to see her, this new
alien creature made from Old World stories, plane
rides, suffering, and luck. She was our first,
the first girl, the first to be grown from here,
not a weed or a stolen vine, not planted from
elsewhere, but rooted, here in this soil. She was
not piecemealed or half-made. This land of misery
and promises would claim her. She was of it.
We held our wonder, imagined the land that would
hold us all now to her. No need for paper, documents
of our naturalized tongues. No more aching
for ground and memory. She would be the new
world. We all saw our bright planet in her small
blue eyes, curly hair. We did not want to see
any accents or sadness. She would be the door,
she would be the gate, she would be the whole
to our brokenness. This is how the muting
continues. We contort. We twist ourselves.
We aspire to quiet spaces in between cracks.
Now she looks for her face in the black and white
pictures in my mother's shoeboxes. *What am I?*
Who am I? she demands. She rages against
the emptiness of bootstraps and hidden shames.
Oh, we try to tell her something of our deep deep
past and sorrow. What the Pacific smells like,
the way to hold her tongue to roll an *R*. How
to eat cebolla y tomate. How to claim more than
this dirt. But we are ghosts. We have given up
the flesh. We are like ghouls after the war.
And she has no patience for quiet immigrants.

AUTHOR'S NOTE

I started writing this book in earnest over five years ago when I was diagnosed with cancer. It was a way to fight off fears of death and pain. But there are so many people and organizations who have nurtured, supported, and believed in my writing. My deepest thanks to Rebecca Morgan Frank, an incredible poet and mentor who gives tirelessly to poetry and poets. Thank you to Sara Rivera and *Grub Street*; I practiced, drafted, wrote and rewrote much of this collection at workshops under your guidance. I would also like to offer my thanks to the Squirrel Hill Poetry Workshop, the poets who were part of an amazing workshop at the Bread Loaf Writers' Conference, and to Canto Mundo and my fellow Canto Mundistas. I have learned so much from you. My sincere thanks to Allegheny College and the Academic Support Committee for funding my sabbatical trip to Chile. I would also like to thank the journals and editors who published many of these poems and took a chance on my writing. I could not have written this book without the love and support of my family and friends—especially un millon de gracias a mi mamá, Macarena, who continues to remind me to write poetry even when I do not think I have any left in me; to my sisters, Montserrat and Javiera, who inspire me every day with their strength and grace; and to my goddaughter Natalia, a poet and artist whose work I cannot wait to read in the future. I would also like to thank my father and my extended family in Chile. This book would not have been possible without my friends, Aimee, Missy, Stephanie, and Barbara, who listened to me complain about rejections and who have been my biggest fans, believing in my work even when I did not (thank you Barbara for publishing my work). And thank you to my chosen brother Amor, who has been on my team since grad school. There are not enough words to thank my beloved, Richard Heppner, my first reader, my best friend, and my heart. This book would not be possible without you. For over twenty-five years, you have supported me, loved me, cared for me, fed me, let me cry, and made me laugh. You have been gentle and you have been strong, even when I did not believe (and still at times do not believe) in my work and words. Finally, I want to thank the artists, activists, writers, leaders, exiled people, and Chileans who believed in a better world and carried so much light in a time of deep suffering and death during the Pinochet years. I was young when I left Chile and learned much of what I write about here from your stories, your words, your lives, and your legacies. I am grateful for you and grateful to you.

BIOGRAPHICAL NOTE

M. Soledad Caballero is a professor of English at Allegheny College. Her scholarly work focuses on British Romanticism, travel writing, postcolonial literatures, WGSS, and interdisciplinarity. She is a CantoMundo fellow, has been nominated for two Pushcart Prizes, has been a finalist for the *Missouri Review*'s Jeffry E. Smith Editors' Prize in poetry, the *Mississippi Review*'s annual Editors' prize, the Lucille Medwick Memorial Award, and the Ruth Stone Poetry Prize. Her poem "Myths We Tell" won the 2019 Joy Harjo Poetry Prize for *Cutthroat: a Journal of the Arts*. She is a co-recipient of a National Endowment for the Humanities Connections Grant, as well as a Great Lakes Colleges Association Expanding Collaborations Initiative Grant. Her first poetry collection won the 2019 Benjamin Saltman Poetry Award sponsored by Red Hen Press. Caballero splits her time between Meadville and Pittsburgh, Pennsylvania.